FARMING
ASSETS

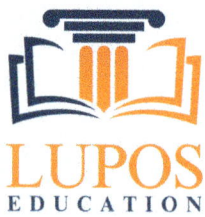

LUPOS

EDUCATION

FARMING
ASSETS

A GUIDE TO GROWING
TAX-FREE CASH FLOW

ROBERT WOLF

Farming Assets: A Guide to Growing Tax-Free Cash Flow
©2023 by Robert R. Wolf

ISBN: 978-1-7331877-1-8 (Paperback)
ISBN: 978-1-7331877-2-5 (eBook)

Library of Congress Control Number: 2023917399

Book Two in The Wolf Financial Trilogy

First Edition
Printed in the United States of America

Editing by Deborah Ager of Radiant Media Labs™, LLC
www.radiantmedialabs.com

Cover Design and Interior Formatting by Becky's Graphic Design®, LLC
www.BeckysGraphicDesign.com

Thank you to my wife Sara for 25 years of marriage and always believing in me. Thank you for my now young adult kids (Isaac, Jordan "Jojo", and Hannah) for blessing our lives.

Table of Contents

Introduction

Imagine you go for a walk and see a pond covered with algae. Gnats form clouds over the surface, and you wrinkle your nose at an unpleasant, bitter odor. The water isn't healthy. However, you can improve the situation if you find a way to add healthy water to the stagnant water. You don't even need the water to be 100% clean and healthy, yet the water *does* need to flow. If you added clean, flowing water into this stagnant pond, the algae would eventually disappear, and the gnats and odor would also disappear.

Cash works in a similar way. Stagnant cash becomes unhealthy, because taxes, inflation, time, laws and regulations, and debt eat away at the money. Each of those areas that "eat" money is what I call an "Economic Termite." And, when there's a healthy influx of cash or what we call "cash flow," the undesirable elements dissipate just as the bugs and odor did in my example.

This book focuses on redirecting your flowing cash into a field that can grow your assets. We have a saying in our firm, "Income is taxable, and cash flow is 'planable.'" We say this, because we focus on what kind of plan you can put in place to allow the flow of cash to grow. Imagine this. If you had a flow of water with no direction or plan, then that water could end up in a street, river, pond, lake, or ocean. River banks keep water heading in the right direction. Water dissipates after spreading. Either the ground absorbs the water or it evaporates. With direction and guidance, you can redirect the flowing water into a field and grow crops as part of a bigger plan to grow and provide food for people. My Asset Buddy System™, which I'll talk about later, provides that same type of direction for my clients.

As with the water analogy, cash that flows with direction and purpose can become more productive. You can direct flowing cash in a way that grows your assets. Grant Cardone, a well-known business development specialist, says that we should *store*–instead of merely *save*–cash. Using the word "store" underscores the point that we want to be able to access and use our cash one day, so we can fund our future. Farmers store crops for later use or sale, and we want to do the same with our own money. For example, even if you had $10,000 stacked on your bedside table, the cash doesn't have value until you use that money to buy a good or service. Inflation causes that amount to be worth less. When you put that $10,000 into an asset, such as real estate, you could have a value worth more than the original amount.

I want to teach you about cash flow and how, given the right purpose, assets can grow and create yet more cash flow. In the following pages, we'll show you how to use multiple assets to develop a plan of creating tax-free income by understanding how assets work–and not just assets but the most tax-efficient assets.

With the water, cash, and farming analogies I've already mentioned, you might understand why I titled this book *Farming Assets*. I am going to be your "Farmer" explaining how to grow assets by directing cash flow in the fields you wish to harvest most. In the real world you would call me an Asset Coach & Tax Strategist™.

Why Read this Book, and How is Our Approach Different?

Since there are thousands, if not millions, of business books out there, why bother with this one? As an avid reader, I have read many myself. As I have read, I sometimes sat there and thought, "Hmm, this was good information. Now what?" or "I'm not sure how this pertains to my situation. It would be great if I could call the author and find out."

Over the last 20 plus years working in my field and helping clients, reading books, attending trainings, and more, I realized I could help people connect their unique situation with the information that would most help them–not just generic ideas. I connect dots to help you reveal the full picture of what to do. With dot-to-dot pictures we may have used as children, you can sometimes guess the full picture without connecting the dots first, because your brain is able to connect the dots based on past experiences. When you *did* draw the line between the dots, the picture would reveal itself to you. Although you already see or know the dots, the full picture isn't revealed until all the dots are successfully connected. The dots have to be connected to create the full picture.

Imagine a bookstore for a moment, and I'll show you what I mean. When you are standing in front of the shelves looking at books filled with strategies, advice, and opinions, you might not know which book will help you. You might not have time to read every book on the topic to find the information or apply that knowledge to your situation. In other words, the dots can't be connected–at least without a significant amount of time spent studying and reading.

Our consulting practice draws from different strategies, so your particular needs can be addressed. Due to our well-rounded experiences, we can tailor our advice to particular needs and goals as opposed to offering the same well-worn advice everyone else offers. Maybe you're wondering how in the world you are going to do this when you don't know me? I will walk you through the considerations.

Who am I?

I began my career in finance with a newspaper route.

Thanks to the newspaper, I could see the stock quotes. This was before the internet existed when we could only find the information in the newspaper.

The stock market information intrigued me, so I began reading books on the topic. Did I enter the world of finance? Nope. In my early 20s, I worked in computer aided drafting, which I'd studied throughout high school. I loved this work. Later, I married and bought a house.

After five or six years into this career, I read a book called *Rich Dad Poor Dad* by Robert Kiyosaki. I admired the way he explained how money worked. He defined how to look at money. More importantly, he showed how to understand the value of assets and liabilities and how both can be valuable if you know what or how to use them. We will go into this more throughout the book.

Since I wanted to read more by Kiyosaki, I read *Rich Dad's CASHFLOW Quadrant*. After reading that book, I told my wife, "I'm quitting my job and looking for a career in finance where I can help people."

Fast forward to 2015-2016. Still married. Three kids. Around this time, I finally became fed up with myself and with the financial planning industry. I was tired of being like everyone else, I had different ideas and strategies to offer and wanted to do this to help people even more than before.

The financial industry teaches us all the same ways, so we become clones offering the same advice. Yet I observed one compelling difference. As I studied top performers in my industry, they had one common element among them besides being successful. They helped clients understand how to minimize their tax liabilities.

As I reflected on the top performers and my past clients, I thought about how clients had frequently complained about taxes. I had given the advice we were taught–whether you are a "financial advisor," money manager, insurance professional, CPA, attorney, etc. Ideas began to click into place. Robert Kiyosaki's books *Rich Dad, Poor Dad* and *Rich Dad's CASHFLOW Quadrant* underscored the importance of the knowledge I wanted to share as part of my work with clients. This led me to the way I perform my work now. I started educating my clients on these two books, and I incorporated strategies I had learned over my long career into my work with clients.

Clients began to see results immediately. They could now understand the game the wealthy play. A big part of the success involves understanding that the tax code was designed for business owners. The US government is a business that runs itself on tax revenue, which is its cash flow. We need to understand how they generate that cash flow.

What to Know About the Government and Taxes

Remember that I said, "Income is taxable and cash flow is planable?" The government taxes income, and assets create that income. If the government wants more revenue, it needs to invest in more assets (tax payers). As a result, the government gives business owners tax credits, incentives, deductions, rebates, and more through the tax code. If a business owner can pay fewer taxes, then they have more cash flow. They usually reinvest that cash flow into their business, which is their baby, and the business grows. As they grow, they hire employees, who pay taxes and create more revenue for the government.

If you and I know the government runs its business on tax revenue and what they can't collect they either borrow or print, then we need to understand how they generate their revenue. Borrowing and printing money is a liability to the government, yet tax revenue is an income stream coming from its various assets. In that mix is you, the individual taxpayer.

The realization above informed my business offerings, including services as an Asset Coach and Tax Strategist™. Kiyosaki's definition of "assets" states that an asset is something that generates cash flow. On Investopedia, we can find this definition:

"An asset is a resource with economic value that an individual, corporation, or country owns or controls with the expectation that it will provide a future benefit. Assets are reported on a company's balance sheet and are bought or created to increase a firm's value or benefit the firm's operations. An asset can be thought of as something that, in the future, can generate cash flow, reduce expenses, or improve sales, regardless of whether it's manufacturing equipment or a patent."[1]

Important definitions

These definitions of terms used here will aid you in understanding the concepts we share in the book.

Liabilities: I will simply use the definition from Investopedia: "A liability is something a person or company owes, usually a sum of money. Liabilities are settled over time through the transfer of economic benefits including money, goods, or services"[2].

Cash flow: For a business everything is about cash flow. Key indicator: Once we have cash flow, what other decisions can we make? To answer that we need to know the different types of income there are. You can use "revenue" in place of "cash flow" but I prefer the term "cash flow," because it usually indicates productivity and control.

1   https://www.investopedia.com/terms/a/asset.asp
2   https://www.investopedia.com/terms/l/liability.asp

Income: The IRS[3] lists of 25 income types in their appropriately named publication "Topic No. 400 Types of Income." I will trim the list down to five. Yes, you are welcome. My "generosity" here is actually self-serving because, if I were to go through that entire list, you would close and shelve this book until your next garage sale if you didn't fall asleep first. The most important key I need you to understand is that cash flow becomes income when it flows down the funnel.

Various types of income:

- Earned Income
- Passive Income
- Active Income
- Investment/Portfolio Income
- Rental Income

Earned Income, according to Investopedia, is "For tax purposes, earned income is any income you receive for work you have done for an employer or a business of your own."

Passive Income and Active Income are describing how income is passed down to your 1040 and if the negative (loss) of these incomes can be deducted from your other positive incomes. When you have assets and there is a year-end where you have a loss, the designation determines if you can deduct that loss. Positive and Negative income is still income when it flows down the Income Funnel.

Passive Income doesn't necessarily go away if you cannot deduct that loss this year. The income gets stored in the loss storage, so to speak, and can be removed if that asset is sold later. If that asset

---

3   https://www.irs.gov/taxtopics/tc400

is sold later and there is a capital gain, meaning you made money, you can use the loss to offset that gain to minimize your tax liability.

Investment/Portfolio Income include earnings generated from investments such as equities or commonly known as the stock market. You can earn dividends, interest, and capital gains which all are taxed differently based on what it is.

Rental Income is income generated from your real estate portfolio. This will be discussed in much more detail later on, but it's important to know that, based on your income amount and your depreciation, we can help designate some of this income as tax free and organize the asset(s) to minimize what would be considered as taxable income.

What is an Asset Coach and Tax Strategist™?

This is someone who helps teach and coach about the various assets available to you and then how those same assets are viewed by the IRS.

Officially, I help teach how to organize your assets to work more efficiently (harder) while receiving additional tax benefits (savings). This causes those same assets to work harder for you, so you can increase your cash flow without increasing unnecessary risk. In order to accomplish this, you need to know:

1. what kind of income you want,
2. how the IRS views each asset, and
3. how the assets you want will accomplish both one and two.

Now, let's get into the specifics of how you being an employee or an employer can affect how much you pay in taxes.

How Employment Status Can Decrease or Increase Your Taxes

The CASHFLOW Quadrant and How It Works

The basics of *Rich Dad's CASHFLOW Quadrant* explains how taxes and income are associated with each other. However, I've redefined some of them to better suit the unique situations of my clients. Let's start with explaining how "E" affects your assets.

In this book, I use "CASHFLOW" when referring to the book by Kiyosaki and "cash flow" everywhere else.

$$
\begin{array}{c|c}
E & B \\
\hline
S & I
\end{array}
$$

The E Quadrant represents the Employee. This person trades time for dollars and earns a wage for that time. The IRS designates that wage as a W2 employee. The W2 form shows these wages as income so, when we look at our Income Funnel, cash flow becomes income by this designation.

The Employee files a personal tax return, the form 1040, and has the choice to "itemize" or take the "standard" deductions. They are limited to tax reductions outside the Schedule A, which allows the employee to "itemize" expenses based on predetermined expenses on the Schedule A.

If, by itemizing, their total is more than the "standard" deduction provided by the IRS, then they can take the greater of the two.

The S Quadrant represents the Self-Employed. Kiyosaki describes a self-employed person as anyone in the service industry such as doctors, CPAs, attorneys, and other similar business professionals. I differ from Kiyosaki on this quadrant. I describe this as the person who has chosen not to set up a separate business entity, which means the income earned is considered self-employed income for which they file a Schedule C. All taxpayers have access to a Schedule C. They are allowed to deduct expenses that are related to them earning self-employed income, yet deductions are limited. They pay higher income taxes, because they also pay a self-employed income tax.

The "E" and "S" quadrants provide a lot of revenue for the IRS. These quadrants are tax-inefficient for you and me and cause us to pay more in taxes than we should

The B Quadrant represents Business. Kiyosaki writes that this designation refers to a 500+ employee business. I have redefined this to include a separate business entity, such as a S-Corp, C-Corp, Partnership. The LLC can designate how they are taxed. .

As a separate business entity, now the tax code opens up. Basically, the IRS rewards you for taking your Self-Employed business from hobby to official status, which suggests to them a higher level of seriousness.

In this quadrant, you get to file not only your business tax return, but you also get to have more of the tax code available to you. If you are building and growing your business and that causes a paper loss, you get to have that loss of income flow down the Income Funnel on your personal tax return on your Schedule 1. The Schedule 1 summarizes the results of all your business entities and corporate tax returns–both positive and negative.

The I Quadrant, which I call the "A" Quadrant, represents Investment. Kiyosaki uses the term "investment," because he is writing a book for the general public and they understand that term. However, he's actually saying that you want to have your money go into "assets." That's why I call this the "A" Quadrant and not the "I" Quadrant.

Assets generate cash flow, which is what every business owner wants. Once we have cash flow, then you can designate how much of that needs to flow down the Income Funnel as income. The key here is to understand what type of income you want: taxable income or tax-free income.

If you had a choice, which would you choose? Taxable income or tax-free income? If you choose "taxable income," you have two options:

1. reevaluate your answer or
2. stop reading and spend your time in the garden.

I'm not joking. This book is for those who are frustrated with taxes and, more importantly, frustrated from not knowing how the system works.

For those who chose tax-free income, the next step is to determine what Assets allow us to have tax-free income as per the IRS. The other determination I will give you is the formula to continue

13

to increase that tax-free income by using the various assets. The most important indicator is in what order those assets need to be in. For example, when you look at a train, the engine is in the front or back and never in the middle. For a train to be effective, the parts have to be in the right order. Based on the assets, you can determine what tax forms and schedules are needed and how to report your dealing to the IRS.

Economic Termites: What "Eats" Your Money?

Question: When do you know you have a
termite problem in a dwelling?
Answer: When the damage has already been done.

The same goes for what I call "economic termites," which happen in our daily economic lives on a macro and micro level and affect our ability to grow our savings and wealth. Five major economic termites exist:

1. Taxes,
2. Inflation,
3. Time,
4. Laws & Regulations,
5. Debt.

To spare you from boredom, I will address these based on an overarching understanding and then address them in more detail from our planning perspective. This will help you get an idea of how to avoid them, so you can grow your assets more efficiently.

The Queen Termite: Laws & Regulations

Before we dive into the two most discussed termites–taxes and inflation, I want to address the worst termite of them all. You could say this is the queen termite.

Laws & Regulations are the worst, because our lawmakers and politicians are the ones who pass laws that affect our wealth. This is not a political conversation. This is a fact. And both parties change and create laws that affect our wealth and future.

In the last decade or two, politicians smartened up (in their mind) and began using the tax code to their advantage when they passed laws. Those decisions either created positive or negative effects but there is balance, so each law linked to the tax code hurts and/or helps us. The government will make a law change or tax benefit. Congress may tell tax payers they made a change to benefit us but then they change something in another area that negatively affects us. We may not know they even made the negative change, because we don't think to look for it and it's buried in pages of dull legal documents. When there are tax changes, some adjustments help business owners even more, because businesses hire employees. But they don't notify us of what they're doing.

Lawmakers create these changes when they need tax revenue to run their own business or line their pockets. This might sound judgmental, yet history backs me up. No public servant should be a multimillionaire on the backs of citizens. I could go on and on about this horrible termite, but the sad thing is you already know what I'm talking about, which means this has become pretty bad. By learning the rules and using those rules to your advantage, you can change the direction of your future the right way!

Taxes[4]

This section will form the foundation of how to achieve a lower taxation in your wealth-building strategy. That means you keep more of your own money–legally. To help explain what taxes are, I will use the Tax Foundation as a resource. The Foundation explains three basic tax types with four categories falling under each type.

1. Taxes on what you earn:

   a. Individual income taxes

   b. Corporate income taxes

   c. Payroll taxes

   d. Capital gains taxes

2. Taxes on what you buy:

   a. Sales taxes

   b. Gross receipts taxes

   c. Value-added taxes

   d. Excise taxes

3. Taxes on what you own:

   a. Property taxes

   b. Tangible personal property taxes

   c. Estate and inheritance taxes

   d. Wealth taxes

---

4   https://taxfoundation.org/the-three-basic-tax-types/

Taxes on What You Earn

According to the Tax Foundation,"half of taxpayers
pay 97 percent of all income taxes."

You can see from the quote above why we want to help you with taxes. Individual income taxes can mean your personal earnings such as wages, salaries, investments, or other forms of income and individual or household earnings. These incomes show up on your personal tax form 1040 lines 1-6. See Exhibit A. Lines 2 and 3 will require Schedule B, see Exhibit B.

Attach Sch. B	2a	Tax-exempt interest	2a		b Taxable interest	2b	
if required.	3a	Qualified dividends	3a		b Ordinary dividends	3b	
	4a	IRA distributions	4a		b Taxable amount	4b	

When you look at this tax form you can make the assumption that the taxes are designed as a "progressive" tax meaning that, as your income increases, so does your tax bracket or percentage of taxes owed.

Corporate Income Taxes

To understand corporate taxes, you need to understand the various types of entities and structures a company can run under. The various types of business entities include:

- Sole Proprietor
- C-Corporation
- S-Corporation
- Partnership
- Limited Liability Company (LLC)

The IRS taxes these entities differently. Therefore, the form of taxes collected are different. For example, a C-Corporation is the only entity that is taxed federally with a separate tax rate, which we call a corporate tax. Many states have a corporate tax rate as well. These taxes are often on profits, but there are some states that tax based on gross revenue.

Sole Proprietor, S-Corporation, Partnership, and Limited Liability Company (LLC) are considered pass through which means the profits or losses are passed through to the individual taxpayers' (owners or partners) return. Please note that an LLC can choose the way they want to be taxed, meaning they could apply to be taxed as a Sole Proprietor (single member), C-Corporation, S-Corporation, or a Partnership. The tax forms filed to the IRS are as follows:

- Sole Proprietor ▶ Form 1040 Schedule C
- C-Corporation ▶ Form 1120
- S-Corporation ▶ Form 1120S
- Partnership ▶ Form 1065
- Limited Liability Company ▶ Depends on what is chosen above since an LLC can choose the form of taxation

Payroll Taxes

These taxes are collected on wages and salaries from the employer and the employee and pay for social insurance programs. These come directly out of each paycheck. Social Security payroll taxes collected a total of 12.4 percent split between employer and employee equally (for now). Medicare payroll taxes collected a total of 2.9 percent split between the employer and the employee equally (for now).

Capital Gains Taxes

These taxes are owed when a gain is realized on an investment. For example, when you purchase certain investments–including stocks, bonds, homes, cars, jewelry, art, and crypto-currencies–the price you pay for it is called your "basis" or "principal." If the asset appreciates–grows to be more than what you paid–then the asset creates what's called a "capital gain." When you sell this asset, you will owe a tax on it based on that gain and not the basis or principal. The tax percentage you pay will depend on your overall income for that year.

These incomes show up on your personal tax form 1040 line 7. (See Exhibit A.) This will require Schedule D. (See Exhibit C.)

| separately, $12,950 | **7** | Capital gain or (loss). Attach Schedule D if required. If not required, check here . . . . . ☐ | **7** | |

As a C-Corporation, you can find yourself in a double taxation situation when it comes to capital gains. A C-Corporation pays corporate income tax and then capital gains tax to the shareholders.

Taxes on What You Buy

This section is mixed with consumption (sales taxes, value-added taxes, and excise taxes) and business revenue (gross receipts taxes).

Sales Taxes: Most sales taxes are state and local driven based on retail sales of goods and services you consume.

Gross Receipts Taxes: This tax is exactly what you think it is. This is a tax on the gross revenue and doesn't take into consideration the profitability of a company. If you are a startup, then this is going to be potentially harmful yet, as a state or local government, I can see the need to make sure you collect taxes to run your municipality.

Value-Added Taxes: This isn't as prevalent in the United States as it is in other countries, so I'm not going to spend any time on this.

Excise Taxes: These taxes to date have been used on goods and services that could be deemed harmful to the public or are broadly used enough to generate more tax revenue. For example, cigarettes, alcohol, and soda are examples of what could be "harmful" to the public and if you choose to consume these goods then you pay more taxes for them.

Another example would be a gasoline tax, which supposedly would cause people to consume less and help fix carbon emissions and curb pollution. I believe in the near future that there will be an excise tax on retirement funds, such as 401K and IRA types of savings.

But what about health care? What about all the other things that the people in power (politicians) consider to be goods and services to be taxed? We will discuss this more when we discuss the termites of Laws and Regulations in more depth.

Taxes on What You Own

These are taxes on things you buy to help make a better life for you and your family in both the short and long terms.

Property taxes are paid by those who own the property and not those who occupy the property. These taxes are very valuable to states and local governments and make up about 30 percent of tax revenue and over 70 percent of local government revenue. These pay for the local services provided such as schools, roads, public services.

Tangible Personal Property Taxes: These taxes are for personal property that can be for both personal use and/or business use. The tax is usually on machinery and other equipment used, which is different from sales taxes.

Estate and Inheritance Taxes: This complex area of tax law has two sides of the equation debated constantly. One side says this tax discourages investment and the other side says, "You have a lot of money and others don't, so the money should be spread around."

When it comes to state or inheritance taxes, the only ones it affects are those that are closest to that limit. As an example, if the estate exemption is $5M–and your parent passes–the first $5M doesn't get taxed. Any money above the $5M would be taxed at 30%. When we have this type of limit, it only affects the people who are closest to that limit. If the estate is at $3M, you don't have to pay the tax. If the estate is $7M, you'll probably hire tax and/or estate professionals to help you pay less.

My opinion is this is poor economic policy. Those that are in lower-economic groups don't need to think about this. Those in the higher-economic tax groups are more focused on hiring their team to help minimize this as much as possible.

Wealth Taxes: This tax is imposed on individuals annually and really is not a United States issue but related to certain countries in Europe, so I won't spend time on this.

How Inflation[5] Reduces Your Buying Power

The government prefers to keep inflation at 2% annually. At the time of this writing, inflation has hit a new 40-year high and is right around the reported number of 8.8%.

In this section, I'll go over:

- What is Inflation and its Cause?
- The Fed and Inflation
- Inflation and Taxes

What is Inflation and Its Cause?

Inflation happens when the cost-of-living increases or the purchasing power decreases due to the goods and services we purchase

---

5   https://taxfoundation.org/tax-basics/inflation/

becoming more expensive. The Tax Foundation says, "Inflation is sometimes referred to as a 'hidden tax,' as it leaves taxpayers less well-off due to higher costs and 'bracket creep' while increasing the government's spending power." This is when you need more income to pay for higher costs of goods and end up in a higher tax bracket if you're able to increase your income.

When there is more money in the system (economy) for the same goods and services, inflation happens. The Consumer Price Index (CPI) tracks inflation, and the Federal Reserve (Fed) controls the purse strings and can either print more money or adjust the cost of money that banks in the Fed system borrow in the form of the Fed Rate. Both of these can occur, and both of these can be reversed to shrink inflation.

The Fed and Inflation

The Fed's inflation goal is 2 percent each year, and they are on record as saying they think this is a healthy goal. Let's see what this means from a numbers perspective. Since variables come into play and we can't control for all of them, please know that this example uses the historical inflation[6] numbers from usinflationcalculator. com for the sake of simplicity.

First, we will look at average historical numbers showing from 1914 to the last 10 years. Below these numbers, we will show the last 30 years which starts in 1992.

Facts:

- According to USinflationcalculator.com, the last time we had close to double digit inflation was in 1979 – 1981 when it was 11.3, 13.5, and 10.3 respectively and then 6.2 in 1982. The next closest was in 1990 it was 5.4.
- In 2021, we hit 4.7 and YTD in 2022 we had in January 7.5, February 7.9, March 8.5, and in April 8.3.

---

6   https://www.usinflationcalculator.com/inflation/historical-inflation-rates/

Historical Inflation Numbers

AVERAGE INFLATION	
10 years	1.89
20 years	2.16
30 years	2.33
40 years	2.78
50 years	3.91
60 years	3.78
70 years	3.70
80 years	3.76
90 years	3.31
100 years	2.82
Since 1914	3.22

LAST 30 YEARS		
YTD	2022	8.1
1	2021	4.7
2	2020	1.2
3	2019	1.8
4	2018	2.5
5	2017	2.1
6	2016	1.3
7	2015	0.1
8	2014	1.6
9	2013	1.5
10	2012	2.1
11	2011	3.2
12	2010	1.6
13	2009	0.4
14	2008	3.8
15	2007	2.8
16	2006	3.2
17	2005	3.4
18	2004	2.7
19	2003	2.3
20	2002	1.6
21	2001	2.8
22	2000	3.4
23	1999	2.2
24	1998	1.6
25	1997	2.3
26	1996	3
27	1995	2.8
28	1994	2.6
29	1993	3
30	1992	3

As an example, let's use $100,000 as current income and assume the Fed inflation goal of 2 percent. Let's assume you are 50 years old and, in 17 years, you plan to retire at age 66, which is when you can start taking social security. By age 66, your income will need to be $140,024, a 40% increase or 2.35% average wage increase. If no increases happen, then your purchasing power reduces to $70,932, a 29% decrease.

YEAR	AGE	ANNUAL INCOME	INFLATION %	INCREASES	DECREASES
1	50	$100,000	2.00%	$102,000	$98,000
2	51	$100,000	2.00%	$104,040	$96,040
3	52	$100,000	2.00%	$106,121	$94,119
4	53	$100,000	2.00%	$108,243	$92,237
5	54	$100,000	2.00%	$110,408	$90,392
6	55	$100,000	2.00%	$112,616	$88,584
7	56	$100,000	2.00%	$114,869	$86,813
8	57	$100,000	2.00%	$117,166	$85,076
9	58	$100,000	2.00%	$119,509	$83,375
10	59	$100,000	2.00%	$121,899	$81,707
11	60	$100,000	2.00%	$124,337	$80,073
12	61	$100,000	2.00%	$126,824	$78,472
13	62	$100,000	2.00%	$129,361	$76,902
14	63	$100,000	2.00%	$131,948	$75,364
15	64	$100,000	2.00%	$134,587	$73,857
16	65	$100,000	2.00%	$137,279	$72,380
17	66	$100,000	2.00%	$140,024	$70,932
18	67	$100,000	2.00%	$142,825	$69,514
19	68	$100,000	2.00%	$145,681	$68,123
20	69	$100,000	2.00%	$148,595	$66,761
21	70	$100,000	2.00%	$151,567	$65,426
22	71	$100,000	2.00%	$154,598	$64,117
23	72	$100,000	2.00%	$157,690	$62,835
24	73	$100,000	2.00%	$160,844	$61,578
25	74	$100,000	2.00%	$164,061	$60,346
26	75	$100,000	2.00%	$167,342	$59,140
27	76	$100,000	2.00%	$170,689	$57,957
28	77	$100,000	2.00%	$174,102	$56,798
29	78	$100,000	2.00%	$177,584	$55,662
30	79	$100,000	2.00%	$181,136	$54,548

You can see how much inflation reduces your buying power. Those who live on fixed incomes, like hourly wage workers, retirees, or even those on government assistance would be greatly affected by this.

Inflation and Taxes

Now, I will show you what this all looks like using the current 2021-2022 tax brackets for federal income tax rates assuming married filing joint (MFJ).

2021-2022 Tax Brackets and Federal Income Tax Rates

Tax Rate	Single Filers	Married filing jointly or qualifying widow(er)	Married filing separately	Head of household
10%	$0 to $9,950	$0 to $19,900	$0 to $9,950	$0 to $14,200
12%	$9,951 to $40,525	$19,901 to $81,050	$9,951 to $40,525	$14,201 to $54,200
22%	$40,526 to $86,375	$81,051 to $172,750	$40,526 to $86,375	$54,201 to $86,350
24%	$86,376 to $164,925	$172,751 to $329,850	$86,376 to $164,925	$86,351 to 164,900
32%	$164,926 to $209,425	$329,851 to $418,850	$164,926 to $209,425	$164,901 to $209,400
35%	$209,426 to $523,600	$418,851 to $628,300	$209,426 to $314,150	$209,401 to $523,600
37%	$523,601 or more	$628,301 or more	$314,151 or more	$523,601 or more

Using the $100,000 income example again, we can see that your tax liability today would be $13,497. Therefore, your net income after taxes would be $86,503. Fast forward to age 66 when you are retiring. Your income needs to be at $140,024 to equal the $100,000 in present dollars. However, your tax liability increases to $22,302 and you have a net income of $117,722.

Inflation can affect your purchasing power (expenses). Let's assume your monthly expenses are $5,000, so that would be $60,000 per year. At a 2 percent inflation rate, your monthly expenses increase to $7,001 or annually to $84,014 by age 66. When we show that side-by-side with your income need, you're looking at an income range of $140,024 to the low side of $70,932 and your expenses in the middle at $84,014.

YEAR	AGE	ANNUAL INCOME	INFLATION %	INCREASES	DECREASES	ANNUAL EXPENSES	INCREASES
1	50	$100,000	2.00%	$102,000	$98,000	$60,000	$61,200
2	51	$100,000	2.00%	$104,040	$96,040	$60,000	$62,424
3	52	$100,000	2.00%	$106,121	$94,119	$60,000	$63,672
4	53	$100,000	2.00%	$108,243	$92,237	$60,000	$64,946
5	54	$100,000	2.00%	$110,408	$90,392	$60,000	$66,245
6	55	$100,000	2.00%	$112,616	$88,584	$60,000	$67,570
7	56	$100,000	2.00%	$114,869	$86,813	$60,000	$68,921
8	57	$100,000	2.00%	$117,166	$85,076	$60,000	$70,300
9	58	$100,000	2.00%	$119,509	$83,375	$60,000	$71,706
10	59	$100,000	2.00%	$121,899	$81,707	$60,000	$73,140
11	60	$100,000	2.00%	$124,337	$80,073	$60,000	$74,602
12	61	$100,000	2.00%	$126,824	$78,472	$60,000	$76,095
13	62	$100,000	2.00%	$129,361	$76,902	$60,000	$77,616
14	63	$100,000	2.00%	$131,948	$75,364	$60,000	$79,169
15	64	$100,000	2.00%	$134,587	$73,857	$60,000	$80,752
16	65	$100,000	2.00%	$137,279	$72,380	$60,000	$82,367
17	66	$100,000	2.00%	$140,024	$70,932	$60,000	$84,014
18	67	$100,000	2.00%	$142,825	$69,514	$60,000	$85,695
19	68	$100,000	2.00%	$145,681	$68,123	$60,000	$87,409
20	69	$100,000	2.00%	$148,595	$66,761	$60,000	$89,157
21	70	$100,000	2.00%	$151,567	$65,426	$60,000	$90,940
22	71	$100,000	2.00%	$154,598	$64,117	$60,000	$92,759
23	72	$100,000	2.00%	$157,690	$62,835	$60,000	$94,614
24	73	$100,000	2.00%	$160,844	$61,578	$60,000	$96,506
25	74	$100,000	2.00%	$164,061	$60,346	$60,000	$98,436
26	75	$100,000	2.00%	$167,342	$59,140	$60,000	$100,405
27	76	$100,000	2.00%	$170,689	$57,957	$60,000	$102,413
28	77	$100,000	2.00%	$174,102	$56,798	$60,000	$104,461
29	78	$100,000	2.00%	$177,584	$55,662	$60,000	$106,551
30	79	$100,000	2.00%	$181,136	$54,548	$60,000	$108,682

When it comes to the rest of the termites, check out my book *Economic Termites*. In this book, *Farming Assets*, my goal is to dive deeper into taxes and inflation.

They say you can't buy time, but you can.

The IRS even shows you how as long as you follow the plan design. The rest of this book will show you what to consider and do.

- How to use debt instead of letting debt use you.
- How the worst termite of them all, Laws & Regulations, affect the other termites and your ability to build wealth.

3

How to Build Your Wealth Using Tax–Free Cash Flow

Most people feel like they are overpaying federal taxes, but they don't know if they actually are, because no one has helped them to calculate what their "fair share" in taxes are. We are not legally required to pay more income taxes than our "fair share." The information shared here will help you see how much you overpay and what to do about it.

Is the IRS The Evil Empire?

The public can search the IRS tax code. In fact, the IRS writes Publications[7] and Bulletins highlighting and explaining in detail what the code allows and how to use it. Like most instruction manuals, we might not know how to implement them even though we can access and read them. The wealthy have tax teams to comprehend the laws and guide them to the best decisions given their situation. The ideal team has expertise in certain areas of the code, whereas

---

7   https://www.irs.gov/publications

any given expert can only provide guidance with part of the picture. You need to have a team that specializes in getting you closer to that "fair share" instead of overpaying. Everyone understands we use public services, so we want to pay our taxes for those. That would be our fair share.

Congress understands that the US economy is run on the backs of small businesses. As a result, the IRS is your business partner in that they provide tax deductions, tax credits, tax incentives, and tax rebates, which are spread all throughout the IRS tax code. They give business owners the opportunities to reduce tax liabilities, and that increases our cash flow. While individual taxpayers also get some of these, they don't receive as many, because tax revenue would decrease too much.

As a business owner, when you have additional cash flow, your business partner (the IRS) knows and understands you are going to distribute that cash flow back into your business to grow it. They know we'll do this, because we have our blood, sweat, and tears invested in our businesses.

As we grow, we can't do all the work ourselves any longer, so we hire employees (W2) or independent contractors (1099). When you hire employees, you pay them a W2 wage, which is exactly the income revenue the IRS is looking to collect. W2 wages provide consistent tax revenue, because the prospect for W2 wage earners to have a plan to lower their tax liability isn't likely. Remember, as we mentioned earlier, the government's tax revenue comes off the backs of wage earners through payroll taxes.

As business owners, we seek consistent revenue, so we can distribute cash flow into our business to grow in a predictable way. The IRS is no different. The US government is a business and needs cash flow, too. When they don't collect enough revenue (taxes), then they have to borrow or print money, and that can cause issues that make politicians unpopular.

Audits: The IRS Ensuring Their Investment Yields Consistent Results

When the IRS receives your financial statement (tax returns) they would like to verify the reporting, so they can make sure their "investment" in you as a business produces consistent results. When we provide financial statements to the IRS, we need to make sure we are documenting and focusing on the purpose of why we have taken tax deductions, tax credits, tax incentives, and tax rebates. Once we prove that we are a good business partner and have reported correctly, the IRS goes on their merry way and we continue to work together.

Although this explanation simplifies the process and actually makes the experience sound pleasant and productive, you'll sometimes find the IRS may be suspicious or intimidating when they do an audit. With that in mind, be sure you document and prove your purpose. You'll be better off if you do. To clarify, the purpose of claiming tax deductions, tax credits, tax incentives, and tax rebates is to protect the partnership between you and the IRS. Protect your partner (the IRS), and they will continue to reward you.

Before we go over the translation of what this means. I'd like to discuss the current formula we have been taught since a young age:

$$I - T - E = S:$$
Income – Taxes – Expenses = Savings

We are taught to get a good education, then get a good "job" to earn a living and make money" and then save for our future.

The formula above shows this clearly: What's left after taxes and expenses is discretionary. When you earn an income, taxes come out first and you have to pay your expenses. At the end of the day, you are left with the crumbs to save. The term "discretionary income" makes us feel better about only having crumbs leftover.

Investopedia has a slightly different definition than mine.: "Discretionary income is the amount of an individual's income

33

that is left for spending, investing, or saving after paying taxes and paying for personal necessities, such as food, shelter, and clothing. Discretionary income includes money spent on luxury items, vacations, and nonessential goods and services."

I want to pull this next part of the definition out separately so we're sure to see exactly what it says:

"Because discretionary income is the first to shrink amid a job loss or pay reduction, businesses that sell discretionary goods tend to suffer the most during economic downturns and recessions." And they also note that, **"discretionary *spending*** is an important part of a healthy economy. People only spend money on things like travel, movies, and consumer electronics if they have the funds to do so."

These definitions say that an economic downturn will negatively affect your lifestyle and fun. Are you ok with this? Is this why you started your business and you work so hard– only for outside events not in your control to ruin your happiness, feeling of contentment or pride in your reward for your hard work? That's why we plan for wealth building.

Planning for Your Wealth Building

When you plan your wealth building, you're essentially controlling the accumulation, preservation, and protection of that wealth.

The three stages of an asset in order are:

1. Contribution (Investment),
2. Accumulation (Growth),
3. Distribution (Income).

The Contribution Stage starts when you contribute (invest or buy) a dollar amount. Once that stage happens, the asset enters Stage 2, which is the Accumulation Stage where the assets begin to compound. By understanding the rules of assets, we can see how they can be enhanced with efficiencies equal to the asset.

The Accumulation Stage tends to be the longest, depending on the overall plan and how an asset is being used within the plan. But, remember, the purpose of an asset is to generate income which can be:

1.   Deferred to allow the growth and compounding of the assets over a designated time period, or

2.   Activated now for the income to allow other assets to accomplish number one.

The distribution stage, which is stage 3, begins once income is activated from an asset. This stage is where income is distributed out of the asset to allow other assets to take full advantage of the Accumulation Stage.

Each asset has a purpose in an overall plan, so the key to an excellent plan is to be able to take advantage of each stage when it is most efficient, which is different with each client and their situation.

When we have a purposeful plan in place, assets respond instead of react. We'll talk more about events that assets and their rules respond to in a later chapter. First, we need to understand how to use this next element as an important tool for your wealth-building strategy. Read on to see what I mean.

4

Introducing the Asset Buddy System™

The formula I'm about to share with you is what the IRS considers the most tax-efficient assets available to accomplish a good partnership in the short and long terms. Disclaimer: If you try to visit the IRS website and search "3Ds" or even the formula, nothing will show up. This concept is the result of my own translation of what the IRS is trying to tell us. Remember, we are not giving tax advice. We are simply translating our understanding of what is being communicated to us, and we are sharing it as education and for that purpose only.

The 3D Formula to Be in Control of Your Cash Flow

$$D + D + D = TFCF$$
(Deductions + Depreciation + Distributions = Tax Free Cash Flow)

Because numerous methods exist, we're going to discuss some of the most tax efficient methods.

Deductions

The first D represents DEDUCTIONS. Your business assets provide the most efficient tax deductions. As we mentioned earlier, the tax code is written to help you as the business owner. When you plan accordingly, you get deductions to help you grow your business.

Depreciation

The asset that provides the most efficient depreciation is REAL ESTATE. The IRS gives us an amazing opportunity to depreciate-not devalue. Your real estate can still grow in value, but you can depreciate it as if it doesn't. In a later chapter, we'll go into more depth on this but, for now, let's give you a high-level explanation using your purchase of an investment property as an example.

Depreciation reflects deterioration of a structure based on a formula provided by the IRS. This means we record the value of the building as though it's degrading over time.

The IRS allows us to expense this value without us adding additional money and, when we perform upkeep on the property, we can deduct that cost as a business expense or even depreciate more depending on what we do to maintain upkeep on the asset.

For all those who understand deductions and depreciation, you are probably saying to yourself, "I can depreciate the machinery in my business." You do have the ability to do that or even other tools or property in your business, but the most efficient is still real estate.

In "Navigating the Real Estate Professional Rules," Tony Nitti, a CPA, wrote that a taxpayer qualifies as a real estate professional if:

"(1) more than one-half of the personal services the taxpayer performs in trades or businesses during the tax year are in real property trades or businesses in which the taxpayer materially participates, and

(2) hours spent providing personal services in real property trades or businesses in which the taxpayer materially participates total more than 750 during the tax year.

A real estate professional taxpayer generally must establish material participation in each rental activity separately. However, the taxpayer may elect to aggregate all of his or her interests in rental real estate for purposes of determining material participation."[8]

Distribution

The whole reason we gather or accumulate assets is to generate income, which Kiyosaki defines as the purpose of an asset. CASH VALUE LIFE INSURANCE does this. We will explain this in more detail later. For now, I'll keep this high-level. The distributions from cash value life insurance can be distributed tax free, and these distributions don't get recognized as "provisional income" or "net investment income tax (NIIT)" by the IRS, because it doesn't get the designation of "income" at all.

The key to what we are talking about is understanding the difference between income and cash flow. If you have seen our Income Funnel explanation at any point, cash flow gets designated as income when that cash flow begins to go down the Income Funnel where it appears on the personal tax return (your 1040).

"Provisional income" or "net investment income tax (NIIT)" exists so Congress can determine the changes to these for tax purposes.

According to Investopedia, "provisional income[9] is an IRS threshold above which social security income is taxable. The base, from Section 86 of the Internal Revenue Code (IRC), triggers the

---

8   Source: https://www.thetaxadviser.com/issues/2017/mar/navigating-real-estate-professional-rules.html

9   https://www.investopedia.com/terms/p/provisional-income.asp

taxability of social security benefits, requiring its inclusion in gross income tax payment on excess amounts. Provisional income is calculated using the recipient's gross income, tax-free interest, and 50% of their Social Security benefits."

Hold on a second. Does that say tax free interest? Do you think with the financial instability the social security fund has experienced that Congress could expand the definition to include "tax free income"? What is net investment income (NII)[10]? According to the IRS, "In general, investment income includes, but is not limited to: interest, dividends, capital gains, rental and royalty income, non-qualified annuities, income from businesses involved in trading of financial instruments or commodities and businesses that are passive activities to the taxpayer (within the meaning of section 469). To calculate your Net Investment Income, your investment income is reduced by certain expenses properly allocable to the income."

Understanding the 3D formula

Deductions + Depreciation + Distribution = Tax Free Cash Flow

You can put the old formula (Income - Taxes - Expenses = Savings) to rest and be in control of your cash flow. That control takes a plan, which we will explain more in the coming pages.

---

10   https://www.irs.gov/newsroom/questions-and-answers-on-the-net-investment-income-tax

Asset Buddy System (Strategy Layering)

The key to our planning model is following the IRS formula of which assets are the most efficient according to the 3Ds. We want to look at what I call the Asset Buddy System, which allows us to layer assets to work with each other rather than individually.

At its core, an asset is something that creates cash flow, which turns into income based on your choice. If we look at assets creating income, we could make the argument that you are also an asset. *You* create income. In fact, you happen to be the only asset of all your assets that has a brain. So, it is your job to tell all your other assets what to do and give them purpose. The best way to understand this is by having your own plan to execute.

This plan is important, which is why I use the 3D strategy for layering. Most clients we work with have an existing business where we are able to help enhance their cash flow by using tax deductions, tax incentives, tax credits, and tax rebates that can shift a portion of the increased cash flow into real estate and cash value life insurance strategies. The amount and percentage is based specifically on each plan.

This section and the 3D section will become more clear as you read on and see what assets we are farming and how, based on the IRS rules and guidelines, each asset is used to help organize and begin the Asset Buddy System and Strategy Layering.

5

Understand How Common Assets Can Form a Strong Plan

"Common assets" is a term I use to describe assets we've usually heard about. My goal here is to review each common asset and use the information shared in this book already to help you understand how these assets work in your overall plan design. This should all be considered as educational and not as advice.

I'm going to share a chart to explain how these assets play by the rules of assets using the three stages. (See Exhibit D.) The chart will indicate if it has a tax benefit in that stage by using a "N" for No or a "Y" for Yes or a "M" for Maybe.

Savings/CDs/Brokerage Accounts

When you make your deposit (contribution) at your local bank or credit union, there is no tax benefit for doing so. As your money sits in this account and earns whatever interest rate (accumulation) that they determine, there is no tax benefit when you withdraw (distribution), because that money is considered discretionary income. In other words, you already paid taxes on this income, and it's extra.

At the end of the year, if you earned any interest, you will receive a 1099 from the bank indicating you earned money above your principal amount. Principal amount means the amount you deposited.

A Certificate of Deposit (CD) works the same way. The difference is with your savings account, because you have the ability to withdraw any amount in the account freely. With a CD, your deposit is locked in for a certain period of time that you choose and the longer your money isn't accessible to you, then typically the more interest you earn.

A brokerage account is a savings type account held at a custodian, such as Fidelity or Charles Schwab. You have the ability to choose the type of investment inside the account to determine the amount of possible rate of return by assessing risk versus reward.

Typically, when you purchase an investment, there isn't a taxable event unless you sell that investment, because that could create a profit or loss that determines your capital gain, which determines your tax liability.

In the chart I say "M" (Maybe) for the Accumulation Stage, because this can accumulate or appreciate until you decide to sell, which triggers the capital gain tax and therefore enters the Distribution Stage. You may be able to earn interest and/or dividends on your investment without having to sell it, which still creates a taxable event but it just wouldn't be a capital gain. It would be considered either interest or dividend income.

Retirement Accounts (401(k), Profit Sharing, Pension Plan, Traditional IRA)

We have available to us a variety of types of retirement accounts, but the main rules are similar which I will explain here and then try to clarify the difference for that specific asset.

A 401(k), profit sharing, and pension plan all can have a contribution made, which is a tax deduction. A Traditional IRA can be deducted as long as some specific rules are met. I will not go that into here since they are easily internet searchable, which is why Exhibit D shows a "M."

They all have the same tax deferral rules meaning after the contribution is made, they can enter the accumulation stage and can grow without taxation.

They also all have the same distribution rules of 59 ½ years old meaning you cannot distribute funds before then. If you do, then there is a 10% penalty on top of the income taxation of the amount distributed.

The money should stay in the account after 59 ½ years old but, if you do not need the funds or do not distribute enough funds annually, you may be required to distribute a minimum amount using a special IRS formula at the age of 72 ½ years old.

This is called Required Minimum Distributions (RMDs) and exists because, in the first two stages, contribution and accumulation, you have not paid any taxes and the IRS will now need some money to give to Uncle Sam. So, at the distribution stage you will pay income taxes and a 10% penalty for the funds not distributed equaling the amount of RMD funds.

Annuity

An Annuity, not in a Traditional IRA plan, does not receive a contribution tax benefit nor distribution tax benefit. The account funds can accumulate without taxation on a deferral basis but again, at time of distribution, can be taxable. One exception is that the amount contributed is considered principal.

Roth IRA

The Roth IRA is one of the only tax-free income benefits available but has limitations in the contribution stage. Typically the only accumulation methods are using the equities markets and the various products and investments surrounding the equities markets.

The contribution has no tax benefits, but the accumulation and distribution stages are both tax advantaged meaning you can grow your account tax free, and you can distribute from your account tax free after age 59 ½ years old or after five years of contributions, whichever is longer. There are no RMDs.

Real Estate

Real estate is a big topic and expands in so many different directions. There are countless books written about this asset class so I'm not going to go into all the different types, ways, or investment strategies to real estate. The goal with this section is to focus on the high-level rules of this asset and the viewpoint from the IRS.

When investing in real estate, outside of a self-directed IRA, there is no initial deduction other than the costs put into upgrading the property from what it was originally listed and purchased as. This means, if you purchased a property and made improvements to the kitchens and bathrooms, then those new costs are deductible–and, in fact, they have the ability to be depreciated.

Depreciation is an expense line item on form Schedule E of the 1040. This is an expense the IRS allows you to take based on formulas and calculations provided by the IRS for certain structures and improvements.

Yes, there is a cost to the material but there is also a depreciated value of that same material. This is why real estate is part of the three Ds and included in the Asset Buddy System.

Once you invest or purchase real estate then the asset can appreciate, and the appreciation is based on the type of real estate it is. For example, a single-family home is valued based on the surrounding comps (comparables) in the area. This means the value is based on similar properties within the area to show the value of the property. In another example, let's say you own an apartment building of 15 units. Usually, there aren't a lot of comparables to pull up, so comps won't be too helpful. So, an appraiser will value the property based on the property value assessed in their experience. This is where having a good appraiser is important but also you need to show what the property was like when you purchased it, and the improvements made to help increase the value. A new coat of paint and some new landscape like adding flowers can make a big difference.

The second stage is appreciation in Real Estate and can be extremely powerful.

The third stage is Distribution and can be immediate and long term. For example, the reason people love real estate so much is because it can generate an income stream on a monthly basis. Using depreciation and structuring the plan correctly, you can generate tax free income. What I see though is most business owners who invest in real estate, invest without a plan and end up generating taxable income which adds fuel to their existing tax problems–too much taxable income.

The last part of real estate takes place when you sell your property and you have the ability to make money off the sale, because this creates a capital gain taxable event. In addition, if you took depreciation expense, then you have to add that back to the gains which causes your capital gain to be higher. To prevent this, you can do a 1031 exchange, which allows you to sell a property and purchase a like or better property without incurring a taxable event.

As you can see, this can get very complicated, but this can all be handled and addressed with a plan.

When you go reference Exhibit D, you will see "N" (no) for tax deduction. Please see the explanation above. You will also see an "M" (maybe) in the accumulation stage and the distribution stage based on what I explained above, as well.

Business

As with the topic of real estate, the business topic can move in several different directions yet, like the real estate section, I'm going to try and keep it focused on the three stages.

Looking at Exhibit D, you see there is a "M" (maybe) for both the contribution stage and the accumulation stage.

You see when you start a business that pretty much everything you put into your business is an expense, which is a deduction. Depending on your business entity structure, you are increasing your cost basis which is another way of saying principal.

Your business can accumulate what is called cash flow and it will generate income (distribution) which is the third stage. You can pay yourself a paycheck or take distributions and, based on the entity, depends on how you are taxed.

I like to say the tax code is written for business owners. If you think about it when it comes to cash flow, then the more cash flow a business owner has the more he can put back into his business to grow yet more cash flow. At some point, when a business grows, the owner just can't do all the work by themselves, so they hire employees–the E Quadrant.

Employees pay income taxes and there are also payroll taxes, which is what the government uses to budget their spending. Well, they used to pay attention to that and now it just seems they spend like they have a money tree, which they do called the Federal Reserve. If an employee pays taxes, then the government is generating revenue which they need. If they need more money for their budget, they borrow or print money.

The tax code helps a business owner grow, which helps the government tax revenue grow. This is what we call a partnership. When a business owner decides to grow his business more, he has the ability to create more deductions because of the expenses used to help grow revenue. The key is how you plan the business cash flow and how to flow cash into tax efficient assets.

Cash Value Life Insurance

This is a term used to describe a life insurance policy that allows for cash to accumulate inside the policy (equity), which is considered both cash value and accumulation value that are tracked.

There are few types of cash value life insurance policies which I will not go into in this book. If you are interested in more information on this topic, please email us at support@terrafirmaconsultantsllc.com so we can send you a video explaining the different types of life insurance policies available.

When reviewing this asset against Exhibit D and the three stages, the benefits are very similar to the Roth IRA. Typically, you cannot deduct premiums to this asset but there are a couple strategies where the IRS does allow for this. Keep in mind if the IRS allows for something like this benefit of a tax deduction, then there may be other designs and/or requirements taking some of the benefit away. For now, in this book, let's just say there is no tax deduction, which is a more conservative approach.

After the contribution has been made, the cash can accumulate income tax free with access to the cash (equity) as it enters into the accumulation stage. In stage three, the distribution stage, you can distribute income without income taxation. In fact, there is no limitation to accessing this cash as long as there is cash available.

What Others Say

I shared the overall viewpoint looking at the three stages, but I think it appropriate to discuss what many in the finance world say about this most amazing asset.

One of the main comments made is this type of policy is expensive and has high fees. That is true, as with anything you buy. You can overpay for anything or over invest in anything. But for some reason I think this particular asset has been harmed by the simple fact of misunderstanding this is an asset and not necessarily just life insurance. Yes, this is life insurance yet–as with the term "real estate"–the words "life insurance" can refer to many things.

Most want to compare cash value life insurance to the true definition of life insurance where you have a policy to pay in the event of your passing, and this does happen with all forms of life insurance. However, this asset gets compared to term life insurance due to the cost.

As with real estate, if you are living in a home that you are renting, the house is still a single-family house. The house doesn't change but the use of it by who is using it changes. The same goes with life insurance. If you have term life insurance, you are renting life insurance which many times is less expensive than cash value life insurance. But it's the use that is different.

I think what would be appropriate here is to give a brief overview explanation of the most recognized types of life insurance before we discuss cash value life insurance and how the IRS views or taxes it compared to the three stages like we have done with the other assets previously discussed.

Term Life Insurance

Term may be the most popular and is certainly the most advertised due to the short term and low expense of it, so advertisers use this to their marketing benefit. The bottom line this form of insurance is temporary and is purchased for a period of time, such as 10-20 years and also is available in up to 30-year increments. Once that period is up, the policy can stay "inforce" (inforce means that the policy is active) but the premiums (costs) go up each year, and it's based on the insurance companies' actuary tables.

If you don't pass away, no return is given. While some companies offer a return of premium, most don't. If a company is going to return money, do you think they'll charge more for that benefit? Yes, of course.

The best way to understand this is by returning to the renting analogy. When you are done renting a place to live, can you go back to the landlord and say, "Ok, can you give me all my money back?" Good luck! Think about how hard it is to get your deposit back.

Permanent Life Insurance

Permanent life insurance, as you can see by the naming of it, is not temporary or like a term life insurance policy. When we say permanent, we are referencing the time period from an actuarial perspective. These policies are designed to age 120 as of this writing. Before 2001 they were designed to age 100. Due to life expectancy, changes needed to be made. These policies can be designed in pretty much any way based on your age, amount of contribution (premium), death benefit, and how you'd like the cash to accumulate inside the policy.

Due to the policy having the ability to accumulate cash, which is why I refer to this as an asset. You can have it accumulate based on interest rates, dividends, separate accounts (mutual fund type), indexing, and other combinations. These policies are very similar to investing in real estate. In fact, they are so close that if you were to switch one asset for another tax free, the IRS has designated codes such as 1031 for real estate and 1035 for insurance contracts.

We design this asset for accumulation, and we dictate this based on you and your planning needs. If you are interested in more information, we have various videos that you can get from us by contacting: support@terrafirmaconsultantsllc.com.

Final Thoughts on Cash Value Life Insurance

When it comes to building your wealth and your assets, it is best to work with those that have an understanding how, holistically, the various assets discussed can help enhance your goals. Cash Value

Life Insurance is so misunderstood because of misinformation or bad experiences, so it tends to affect the decisions of those looking to grow their wealth.

Based on the three stages, this asset like real estate can have each stage be tax efficient if designed correctly. But for simplicity purposes, looking at Exhibit D, you see that like the Roth IRA, you don't get a tax deduction (the IRS does have a certain design to allow for this, but this is higher level than this book) for your initial contribution.

But when you enter the accumulation stage and begin the distribution stage you are able to have tax-free benefits. Unlike the Roth IRA there are minimal limitations for contributions, income or when you have access to the equity within the policy.

Addendum: Entities

By entities, I'm referring to the business structure of a business. A few of these I mentioned earlier, and I'll define a few additional types here.

- Sole Proprietor
- C Corporation (C-Corp)
- S Corporation (S-Corp)
- Partnership
- Limited Liability Company (LLC)

Please understand this is for educational purposes and is not to be considered advice as to which entity is better than the other. You should seek legal and/or tax advice.

Sole Proprietor

This entity is probably the most common and easiest to set up and run. All you have to do is offer a product or service and charge for it. When you receive payment, you are now considered in business. Estimates suggest more than 30 million of these types of businesses exist. In fact, most recently, the IRS figured out a way to report on these types of businesses by suggesting the banks and financial processors report any revenue over $600 a year as income.

These businesses will file their taxes on the individual owner's personal tax return 1040 using Schedule C.

C Corporation (C–Corp)

This is a "true" corporation. By that, I mean the C-Corp files and pays taxes on the results of profit or loss of the corporation. When you look at public companies, they file as a C-Corp since you can have an unlimited number of shareholders (owners). Depending upon how a C-Corporation is used, it could receive more tax benefits than the other forms or entities, but it pays taxes on its profits. The C-Corp files a 1120 tax return and pays its own corporate tax rate separate from the shareholders tax rates.

S Corporation (S–Corp)

This is a hybrid, called a pass-through, meaning it receives some of the benefits of a corporation but, instead of the corporation paying its own taxes for profit, the profit flows from the S-Corp tax return to the individual shareholders and their personal tax returns. They pay tax rates based on their individual tax rate–not a separate corporate tax rate.

The S-Corp files a 1120S tax return and does not pay its own corporate tax rate, but profits flow from the 1120S to the shareholder's tax rates.

Partnership

A Partnership is an entity designed for separate relationships to share in the ownership of a business and can be another entity and not necessarily a person. There are a variety of structures of a partnership which we will not go into here.

From a tax perspective a Partnership is also a pass through, which means any profits or losses flow to the tax return of the respective partners.

The Partnership files a 1065 tax return and does not pay its own corporate tax rate, but profits flow from the 1065 to the partners tax rates.

Limited Liability Company (LLC)

A Limited Liability Company is a hybrid from a corporation structure and a partnership structure. In fact, you can choose how you wish to be structured and taxed, which can be any of the previous entities and their form of taxation.

Trusts

This is a legal structure to separate other entities and assets based on the desire of the person(s) setting up the Trust. There are different types which I will not go into, yet I thought it appropriate to bring up since it is used as a legal structure.

Thoughts

Based on the guidelines of the IRS code, there is the potential need for a plan to use multiple types of entities due to how the assets and plan of the assets are to be used and how the IRS taxes them. I recommend engaging a tax attorney and consider engaging one who understands estate laws as well.

This leads to the topic of compliance.

Compliance

Compliance is a crucial topic and should be addressed. Anyone looking to develop a plan of action to help accumulate, preserve, maintain, and protect assets should understand the basics of compliance.

I have a very simple way to explain compliance. You should do whatever is necessary to document and prove what you are trying to do and the motivation to execute your plan.

The mindset should be if I am asked a question, can I answer it and have documentation to prove my answer.

The IRS uses the term "reasonable" throughout the code. What does the word "reasonable"[11] mean?

- Not extreme or excessive, moderate, fair, and possessing sound judgment,
- Documenting the idea to prove what you are trying to do is reasonable.

A key point to make here is anytime you are dealing with the IRS, it is good practice to make the assumption that any vague word or phrase is there for you to reasonably define first. This way, if you have to justify your plan, you have defined what was reasonable to you. If you do not take this approach, then the IRS will define your plan from their viewpoint which most likely won't be in line with what your plan was designed to do. Basically, you can set the rules of the discussion and enter more of a level playing field.

Business Protection Program™

Having said all this, I have designed a program to help assist business owners in this area, called the Business Protection Program™.

You see many business owners go about their days assuming the various professions in their lives are helping them in their respective areas of expertise. Yet what happens when there are areas we call "gaps"? For example, what if you had some bricks and you stacked them? Then someone comes over and pushes them and

---

11   https://www.merriam-webster.com/dictionary/reasonable

they topple over. Now, what would happen if in the same scenario each brick had cement mortar connecting each brick to the others. Could that same person push over the couple bricks as last time? No! Think of each brick as your current professional helping in taxation, law, finance, insurance, etc. The Business Protection Program™ is the cement mortar connecting the bricks together.

Rather than me explaining this program in this book, please contact us at support@terrafirmaconsultantsllc.com.

Addendum: Financial Distributors

Financial distributors include banks, investment companies, and insurance companies.

Banks represent leverage meaning we use banks to borrow money to be able to leverage the financing to enhance our purchasing of assets. The normal structure is that we qualify (based on the bank's underwriting guidelines) for financing and, in exchange, we pay principal and interest over an agreed upon time frame.

The key or goal is to have the asset to generate enough cash flow to pay for the costs of borrowing the money and have some leftover. This amount leftover goes by many names, including "positive income" or "positive cash flow."

According to the Federal Reserve[12], before March 2020, banks were required to hold in reserve at least 10% if the "net transaction accounts" amount was over $122.3 million as of 01/18/2018 (as per the Federal Reserve website). What this means is if a bank has to hold cash and is not able to lend it out, then it is considered a liability on the financial statement for the banking institution.

---

12   https://www.federalreserve.gov/monetarypolicy/reservereq.htm

On March 15, 2020, they announced the requirement was reduced down to 0% effective as of March 26, 2020. See below.

LIABILITY TYPE[1]	REQUIREMENT	
	% OF LIABILITIES	EFFECTIVE DATE
Net transaction accounts	0	3/26/2020
Nonpersonal time deposits	0	12/27/1990
Eurocurrency liabilities	0	12/27/1990

Investment Companies represent risk meaning we "invest" our money into these financial instruments, usually some form of stocks, bonds, mutual funds or other similar financial instruments. We weighed the potential "risk vs reward" based on either our understanding or someone else's professional advice.

Vanguard[13] uses a disclosure, which states, "The performance data shown represent past performance, which is not a guarantee of future results. Investment returns and principal value will fluctuate so that investors' shares, when sold, may be worth more or less than their original cost. Current performance may be lower or higher than the performance data cited. Get details on the fund's performance, including standardized returns as of the most recent quarter-end."

Insurance Companies represent safety meaning we use these companies to provide financial stability to our overall financial plan. The structure of insurance companies is to provide protection for businesses and personal needs. Each state regulates the insurance industry and have come together to create an association called the National Association of Insurance Commissioner (NAIC)[14]. They set guidelines that cross state borders but ultimately each commissioner in each state has the final word in its state.

---

13   https://investor.vanguard.com/mutual-funds/profile/VFINX
14   https://www.naic.org/documents/industry_ucaa_chart_min_capital_surplus.pdf

Let's take life insurance in California as an example. According to their required minimum capital of $2,250,000, a company is required to have a surplus of 100% of capital. This means they need to have money to pay future claims, so the surplus needs to be accessible. Now, they are allowed to invest the funds. While there are formulas and percentages of risk vs reward, they can consider the returns they earn as investment income. Typically, that is a non-taxable event.

For example, all homeowner's insurance for Allstate will be in the same pool and won't be commingled with the auto insurance. Before there are claims paid on your policy, they are putting the money into reserves. They are allowed to invest this. Warren Buffet calls it "insurance float." They get to invest it and earn a rate of return to offset their expenses. If they don't have a lot of expenses or claims are low, they get to keep that. Buffet increased his wealth when he realized he had access to the reserves to invest and grow money.

When you look at all three of the financial distributors you can see why it is important to have a plan that incorporates each of them. Let me say this in a different way. Each of these distributors use each other's products and services. Banks are one of the number one purchasers of cash value life insurance.

Exhibit A: Form 1040

Form 1040 — Department of the Treasury—Internal Revenue Service
U.S. Individual Income Tax Return **2022** OMB No. 1545-0074 IRS Use Only—Do not write or staple in this space.

Filing Status
Check only one box.
☐ Single ☐ Married filing jointly ☐ Married filing separately (MFS) ☐ Head of household (HOH) ☐ Qualifying surviving spouse (QSS)

If you checked the MFS box, enter the name of your spouse. If you checked the HOH or QSS box, enter the child's name if the qualifying person is a child but not your dependent:

Your first name and middle initial	Last name		Your social security number
If joint return, spouse's first name and middle initial	Last name		Spouse's social security number

Home address (number and street). If you have a P.O. box, see instructions.		Apt. no.	**Presidential Election Campaign**
City, town, or post office. If you have a foreign address, also complete spaces below.	State	ZIP code	Check here if you, or your spouse if filing jointly, want $3 to go to this fund. Checking a box below will not change your tax or refund.
Foreign country name	Foreign province/state/county	Foreign postal code	☐ You ☐ Spouse

Digital Assets
At any time during 2022, did you: (a) receive (as a reward, award, or payment for property or services); or (b) sell, exchange, gift, or otherwise dispose of a digital asset (or a financial interest in a digital asset)? (See instructions.) ☐ Yes ☐ No

Standard Deduction
Someone can claim: ☐ You as a dependent ☐ Your spouse as a dependent
☐ Spouse itemizes on a separate return or you were a dual-status alien

Age/Blindness You: ☐ Were born before January 2, 1958 ☐ Are blind **Spouse:** ☐ Was born before January 2, 1958 ☐ Is blind

Dependents (see instructions):
If more than four dependents, see instructions and check here . . ☐

(1) First name Last name	(2) Social security number	(3) Relationship to you	(4) Check the box if qualifies for (see instructions):	
			Child tax credit	Credit for other dependents
			☐	☐
			☐	☐
			☐	☐
			☐	☐

Income

Attach Form(s) W-2 here. Also attach Forms W-2G and 1099-R if tax was withheld.

If you did not get a Form W-2, see instructions.

1a	Total amount from Form(s) W-2, box 1 (see instructions)	1a	
b	Household employee wages not reported on Form(s) W-2	1b	
c	Tip income not reported on line 1a (see instructions)	1c	
d	Medicaid waiver payments not reported on Form(s) W-2 (see instructions) . . .	1d	
e	Taxable dependent care benefits from Form 2441, line 26	1e	
f	Employer-provided adoption benefits from Form 8839, line 29	1f	
g	Wages from Form 8919, line 6	1g	
h	Other earned income (see instructions)	1h	
i	Nontaxable combat pay election (see instructions)	1i	
z	Add lines 1a through 1h	1z	

Attach Sch. B if required.

2a	Tax-exempt interest . . .	2a		b	Taxable interest	2b
3a	Qualified dividends . . .	3a		b	Ordinary dividends . . .	3b
4a	IRA distributions	4a		b	Taxable amount	4b

Standard Deduction for—
- Single or Married filing separately, $12,950
- Married filing jointly or Qualifying surviving spouse, $25,900
- Head of household, $19,400
- If you checked any box under Standard Deduction, see instructions.

5a	Pensions and annuities . .	5a		b	Taxable amount	5b
6a	Social security benefits . .	6a		b	Taxable amount	6b
c	If you elect to use the lump-sum election method, check here (see instructions) . . . . . ☐					
7	Capital gain or (loss). Attach Schedule D if required. If not required, check here . . . . . ☐				7	
8	Other income from Schedule 1, line 10				8	
9	Add lines 1z, 2b, 3b, 4b, 5b, 6b, 7, and 8. This is your **total income**				9	
10	Adjustments to income from Schedule 1, line 26				10	
11	Subtract line 10 from line 9. This is your **adjusted gross income**				11	
12	**Standard deduction or itemized deductions** (from Schedule A)				12	
13	Qualified business income deduction from Form 8995 or Form 8995-A				13	
14	Add lines 12 and 13				14	
15	Subtract line 14 from line 11. If zero or less, enter -0-. This is your **taxable income**				15	

For Disclosure, Privacy Act, and Paperwork Reduction Act Notice, see separate instructions. Cat. No. 11320B Form **1040** (2022)

Exhibit B: Schedule B, Form 1040

SCHEDULE B (Form 1040) Department of the Treasury Internal Revenue Service	**Interest and Ordinary Dividends** Go to *www.irs.gov/ScheduleB* for instructions and the latest information. **Attach to Form 1040 or 1040-SR.**	OMB No. 1545-0074 20**22** Attachment Sequence No. **08**
Name(s) shown on return		Your social security number

Part I **Interest** (See instructions and the Instructions for Form 1040, line 2b.) **Note:** If you received a Form 1099-INT, Form 1099-OID, or substitute statement from a brokerage firm, list the firm's name as the payer and enter the total interest shown on that form.	**1**	List name of payer. If any interest is from a seller-financed mortgage and the buyer used the property as a personal residence, see the instructions and list this interest first. Also, show that buyer's social security number and address:		**Amount**
			1	

	2	Add the amounts on line 1	**2**	
	3	Excludable interest on series EE and I U.S. savings bonds issued after 1989. Attach Form 8815	**3**	
	4	Subtract line 3 from line 2. Enter the result here and on Form 1040 or 1040-SR, line 2b	**4**	

Note: If line 4 is over $1,500, you must complete Part III.

Part II **Ordinary Dividends** (See instructions and the Instructions for Form 1040, line 3b.) **Note:** If you received a Form 1099-DIV or substitute statement from a brokerage firm, list the firm's name as the payer and enter the ordinary dividends shown on that form.	**5**	List name of payer:		**Amount**
			5	

	6	Add the amounts on line 5. Enter the total here and on Form 1040 or 1040-SR, line 3b	**6**	

Note: If line 6 is over $1,500, you must complete Part III.

Part III **Foreign Accounts and Trusts** **Caution:** If required, failure to file FinCEN Form 114 may result in substantial penalties. Additionally, you may be required to file Form 8938, Statement of Specified Foreign Financial Assets. See instructions.		You must complete this part if you **(a)** had over $1,500 of taxable interest or ordinary dividends; **(b)** had a foreign account; or **(c)** received a distribution from, or were a grantor of, or a transferor to, a foreign trust.		Yes	No
	7a	At any time during 2022, did you have a financial interest in or signature authority over a financial account (such as a bank account, securities account, or brokerage account) located in a foreign country? See instructions			
		If "Yes," are you required to file FinCEN Form 114, Report of Foreign Bank and Financial Accounts (FBAR), to report that financial interest or signature authority? See FinCEN Form 114 and its instructions for filing requirements and exceptions to those requirements			
	b	If you are required to file FinCEN Form 114, list the name(s) of the foreign country(-ies) where the financial account(s) are located:			
	8	During 2022, did you receive a distribution from, or were you the grantor of, or a transferor to, a foreign trust? If "Yes," you may have to file Form 3520. See instructions			

For Paperwork Reduction Act Notice, see your tax return instructions.   Cat. No. 17146N   **Schedule B (Form 1040) 2022**

Exhibit C: Capital Gains and Losses

SCHEDULE D (Form 1040)	**Capital Gains and Losses**	OMB No. 1545-0074
	Attach to Form 1040, 1040-SR, or 1040-NR.	**2022**
Department of the Treasury Internal Revenue Service	Go to *www.irs.gov/ScheduleD* for instructions and the latest information. Use Form 8949 to list your transactions for lines 1b, 2, 3, 8b, 9, and 10.	Attachment Sequence No. **12**

Name(s) shown on return	Your social security number

Did you dispose of any investment(s) in a qualified opportunity fund during the tax year? ☐ Yes ☐ No
If "Yes," attach Form 8949 and see its instructions for additional requirements for reporting your gain or loss.

Part I Short-Term Capital Gains and Losses—Generally Assets Held One Year or Less (see instructions)

See instructions for how to figure the amounts to enter on the lines below. This form may be easier to complete if you round off cents to whole dollars.	(d) Proceeds (sales price)	(e) Cost (or other basis)	(g) Adjustments to gain or loss from Form(s) 8949, Part I, line 2, column (g)	(h) Gain or (loss) Subtract column (e) from column (d) and combine the result with column (g)
1a Totals for all short-term transactions reported on Form 1099-B for which basis was reported to the IRS and for which you have no adjustments (see instructions). However, if you choose to report all these transactions on Form 8949, leave this line blank and go to line 1b .				
1b Totals for all transactions reported on Form(s) 8949 with **Box A** checked				
2 Totals for all transactions reported on Form(s) 8949 with **Box B** checked				
3 Totals for all transactions reported on Form(s) 8949 with **Box C** checked				

4 Short-term gain from Form 6252 and short-term gain or (loss) from Forms 4684, 6781, and 8824 . .	**4**	
5 Net short-term gain or (loss) from partnerships, S corporations, estates, and trusts from Schedule(s) K-1	**5**	
6 Short-term capital loss carryover. Enter the amount, if any, from line 8 of your **Capital Loss Carryover Worksheet** in the instructions	**6**	( )
7 **Net short-term capital gain or (loss).** Combine lines 1a through 6 in column (h). If you have any long-term capital gains or losses, go to Part II below. Otherwise, go to Part III on the back	**7**	

Part II Long-Term Capital Gains and Losses—Generally Assets Held More Than One Year (see instructions)

See instructions for how to figure the amounts to enter on the lines below. This form may be easier to complete if you round off cents to whole dollars.	(d) Proceeds (sales price)	(e) Cost (or other basis)	(g) Adjustments to gain or loss from Form(s) 8949, Part II, line 2, column (g)	(h) Gain or (loss) Subtract column (e) from column (d) and combine the result with column (g)
8a Totals for all long-term transactions reported on Form 1099-B for which basis was reported to the IRS and for which you have no adjustments (see instructions). However, if you choose to report all these transactions on Form 8949, leave this line blank and go to line 8b .				
8b Totals for all transactions reported on Form(s) 8949 with **Box D** checked				
9 Totals for all transactions reported on Form(s) 8949 with **Box E** checked				
10 Totals for all transactions reported on Form(s) 8949 with **Box F** checked				

11 Gain from Form 4797, Part I; long-term gain from Forms 2439 and 6252; and long-term gain or (loss) from Forms 4684, 6781, and 8824	**11**	
12 Net long-term gain or (loss) from partnerships, S corporations, estates, and trusts from Schedule(s) K-1	**12**	
13 Capital gain distributions. See the instructions	**13**	
14 Long-term capital loss carryover. Enter the amount, if any, from line 13 of your **Capital Loss Carryover Worksheet** in the instructions	**14**	( )
15 **Net long-term capital gain or (loss).** Combine lines 8a through 14 in column (h). Then, go to Part III on the back	**15**	

For Paperwork Reduction Act Notice, see your tax return instructions. Cat. No. 11338H Schedule D (Form 1040) 2022

Exhibit D: Chart of the 3 Stages of an Asset

	CONTRIBUTION	ACCUMULATION	DISTRIBUTION
Savings Account	N	N	N
Certificate of Deposit (CD)	N	N	N
Brokerage Account	N	M	N
401(K)	Y	Y	N
Profit Sharing	Y	Y	N
Pension Plan	Y	Y	N
Traditional IRA	M	Y	N
Annuity	N	Y	N
Roth IRA	N	Y	Y
Real Estate	N	M	M
Business	M	M	N
Cash Value Life Insurance	N	Y	Y

Y=Yes   M=Maybe   N=No

BONUS CONTENT!

Please enjoy this excerpt from my first book:
Economic Termites: Protect Your Assets
from Financial Destruction

A Financial Story of Two Brothers

As I mentioned in the beginning of the book, I read hundreds of books and especially enjoyed the ones more technical in nature. Other times, I liked books that told a story to convey the message, which is what this section of my book does. If you already read section one [of Economic Termites]*, you'll probably feel that I'm repeating myself here. And I am. However, I encourage you to read through this part anyway and allow the information to sink in a second time.*

Sam was having a hard time getting ahead financially and emailed his brother about his worries. His brother suggested they meet up in person at their favorite restaurant.

"I'll treat," Jim said.

Sam jumped at the offer. For the past two years, Sam and Jim had barely had time for conversation beyond small talk. They'd been busy with life, family, and work.

In the past, Jim never paid for anything. Sam didn't want to pass up on the opportunity to spend time with his brother while enjoying a free meal. As he entered the restaurant, Sam spotted his brother at the back and joined him at the table. Jim smiled when he saw Sam and stood up to hug him.

As they hugged, Sam noticed Jim seemed happier and more at ease than the last time they'd seen each other, and he hoped to learn his secret. They ordered their meal and a couple of drinks.

"Tell me what's going on, Sam. Your last few emails concerned me. Your tone and energy really seemed low."

"I'm not sure where to start." Sam frowned and shook his head slightly.

"Where do you feel is the start?"

"Well, I feel like I can't get traction. We have a successful business, yet it seems every year we fall farther behind. On the plus side, we have been able to save money in our company 401(k) and buy a few rental properties."

Jim nodded and sipped his drink. The ice clinked in the glass as he set it back on the table.

"We have been working with a financial advisor, but it just seems like we get the same standard information. We asked our CPA for help, and we don't get the advice we need to change things. Each year, we owe more in taxes than the year before," Sam said.

"That's hard," Jim said.

"I'm just not sure how much longer I can work this hard and have the same results."

"I know how you feel, Sam."

"You do?"

"Yep. A few years ago, we had the same frustration. We found a consulting firm that educated us on what they call 'Asset Building.' They taught us that each asset has rules, and we can make educated financial decisions if we understand the rules."

Sam took a bite of his steak and kept listening.

"They taught us the basics, which I initially thought was a waste of time. I almost gave up! As we went through their education, we found it was important because everything ties together.

They taught us to look at things from the IRS's point of view and to understand what they've provided as guidelines."

"Jim, what are you talking about?"

"Ok, Sam, we should begin at the beginning." Jim set his fork down and pulled a notebook out of his pocket. He ripped out some pieces of paper.

"The beginning would be ideal. I need the basics," Sam replied.

"The key to everything is cash flow. That means understanding how cash flows and the consequences of the flow. Will it be taxable or tax free?"

"Wait a second." Sam's eyes grew wide. "Are you telling me there is a way to get tax-free cash?! This doesn't seem to be honest. What have you gotten yourself into?"

Jim laughed. "I said the *exact* same thing! Let me continue, and it will all be clear. Trust me. You know who Robert Kiyosaki is? The author of *Rich Dad Poor Dad*?"

Sam nodded and said, "I read the book years ago. I really like the way he explained the difference between both dads."

"Yes, exactly. He wrote another book called *Cashflow Quadrant*. He explains the difference between the various ways to earn income." Jim sketched the quadrant out on the paper, and Sam leaned closer to look at the drawing.

Jim explained the ideas behind Kiyosaki's book and where they fell in the quadrant. "You and I, as business owners, are in the B Quadrant. Since you own a couple of rental properties, you are also in the I Quadrant (investor). What I found out was that I wasn't thinking like a B or I Quadrant. I had been thinking like an E Quadrant or an employee," Jim said.

Jim described the necessity of increasing assets and using a business, along with the tax incentives we get as business owners, to enhance our Asset Building.

"Since creating more income is the key to being able to compound your overall asset portfolio, we all want to increase our assets. The firm I work with has one goal: to increase my cash flow. They taught me how to increase our B & I quadrants because those quadrants are the two most tax efficient."

Sam nodded, trying to take in all the information his brother was sharing.

"Plus, the IRS wants us to increase those quadrants, which is why they created them to be more tax efficient in the first place."

"That makes sense. Tell me more about making my business more tax efficient," Sam said.

"No, it isn't about making your business more tax efficient. It already is."

"Oh," Sam said. He took a drink.

"It's about understanding the rules of your assets and making them more efficient—not just taxwise but while compounding. Besides you, your business is the greatest asset you have. Does that make sense?"

"Yes," Sam said.

Jim added that Sam should follow certain rules when it comes to assets and financial health. Sam was quickly writing down as much as he could.

Jim waited for him to catch up before continuing. "A book called   describes seven rules that each asset should incorporate.

The book offers a simple message, and the simplest idea often has the biggest impact."

Sam looked up from his notes. "What are the rules?"

"Rule one is to pay yourself first. This rule needs no explanation, but I didn't pay attention to it for some reason. I had been conditioned to pay my expenses first due to the fear instilled in me over losing this or that. You remember when you first started your business? We focused on survival. Since there wasn't extra revenue to save, the expenses were the first to be paid. But now that we have passed that stage, following this rule is vital."

"I remember that about expenses," Sam said.

"And do you remember I said before that I was still in the E Quadrant and thinking like an employee? This is an example. Paying yourself first is the way you can increase your chances of getting into the I Quadrant," Jim said.

"What are examples of paying yourself first? Are you talking about putting money aside each month in my bank savings account?"

"Good question. As an employee, you contribute to your company's 401(k) plan and to your house through your mortgage payments. I did this and so did you. As I learned more, I found these both are not efficient. For now, let's just say you and I, as business owners, can save in better ways for ourselves first."

Sam wrote down a note to ask about this later.

Jim continued, *"The second rule is to control your spending.* Even though I own my own business, I was less diligent in this rule than I thought I was. I found that I was taking more income from my business than I needed and was causing my tax bill to be too high. From the consultants, I learned I should look at my taxes as an expense like all my other expenses. I reviewed my expenses and found I was spending more money than I needed to in order to write them off as tax deductions to save on taxes—not realizing I was throwing money away."

Sam replied, "You know I find it funny you say that because I do the same thing with my spending. When I talk to my CPA—which isn't much—I hear I need more deductions. I spend more to get them."

Jim laughed. "I did the same. That's why I'm walking you through these rules. This is your money. Wouldn't you want to keep it rather than give it away?"

"Of course!" Sam said. "You know, we get trained somehow to do things with really no thought to it. Kind of makes me mad."

The waitress came by and told the brothers that she was going on break and introduced them to her replacement. They ordered dessert.

Sam finished his drink, and Jim started talking again.

"The third rule is to earn a fair rate of return. I wasn't focused on that at first. Every time I talked with my financial advisor, he would always focus on the rate of return and how we should shift investments to do this and that, but I found I wasn't earning more as a result."

The server set two pieces of pie on the table and left.

"In fact, I felt I was losing money," Jim said, slicing into his pie. "In 2008, when the market took that big drop, I lost a lot of money. That took my sights off rule number one. At that point, the last thing I wanted to do was put more money into that rabbit hole."

Sam ate some of his pie and took notes.

"This rule is related to the old story about the tortoise and the hare. Why was I in such a hurry when it came to growing assets? Growing my assets faster than I should, depending on the asset, meant I was taking on more risk and uncertainty than I may have realized."

"I get it," Sam said.

"If we developed a plan to save on taxes, then that was my rate of return. I was in the 37% tax bracket. By implementing certain strategies using the IRS code, I could lower my income to the 32% tax bracket. More importantly, the money saved was like a 37% or

35% rate of return. If I didn't save that money, it would go to the IRS. With that savings, I was able to hire a new salesperson who has paid for herself and then some."

"Wow," said Sam. "That's impressive."

"I know! Let me have some more of this pie." Jim took a bite and looked off into the distance.

"It's good," Sam said. "Just like Grandma's!"

"That's what I was just thinking. Blueberry pie is my favorite." Jim took another bite and smiled. "All right, back to work here. I learned we can grow assets without increasing risks and uncertainty. In fact, don't increase your risk. By taking on more risk, people fall into the trap of the next rule."

Sam's forehead wrinkled in surprise because he hadn't had anyone look at what it meant to earn a rate of return. "You know, we see and hear so much about the stock market on TV that you just subconsciously think about stock investing."

"I know," Jim said.

"That makes sense that I should treat saving on taxes as a rate of return. What is rule four then?"

"Rule number four is don't lose money. This rule seemed to be common sense, but I realized we had leaky faucets everywhere in both personal and business finances. The amount of money lost was crazy. Losing money comes in all forms."

"For example, paying for things we don't use would be a leak, right?"

"Exactly. We looked at whether we were paying too much in credit card interest, spending on products and services that I don't use (gym memberships), or buying products before we'd done enough research on our needs. A dripping faucet is annoying but usually does not receive the attention it deserves until the problem gets out of hand."

"I can't believe what I've been wasting," Sam said. He put his hand on his forehead and shook his head. "This stuff is common sense, but I know I haven't thought about it. I know the other business owners I meet with regularly haven't either. We all complain about the same stuff. But we don't talk about this. I guess when you look at $30 here and $50 there, it doesn't look like much until you add it all up."

"You're right. At least you can do something about it now. In our case, we sat down and added up all the little expenses and found we were spending money like crazy and didn't even realize it. Did we really need Hulu, Netflix, and Amazon Prime accounts plus our normal cable costs? That alone was over $300 a month."

"Yeah," Sam said. "It really does add up quickly."

"But here's the crazy thing—where does the $300 come from?

"From my checking account."

"That's right. Now how did that money get into your checking account?"

"My paycheck," Sam said.

"And what happens to that money?" Jim leaned forward and smiled because he knew Sam would light up when he understood.

Sam's eyes grew wide, and he smiled as he realized the answer.

Jim could tell his brother understood. "It's taxed as income and then goes into your checking account. If the amount is $300, then that means it really is $461 taxed at your federal tax bracket of 35% to net $300 out the door."

"Whoa. What a way to look at it. That means all my personal expenses need to be looked at from that perspective."

Jim nodded. *"Rule number five is to own real estate.* Well, it actually says to make your house a profitable investment. Robert Kiyosaki wrote that your house is not an investment. An investment is something that generates income for you, and your house doesn't do that."

Sam had finished his pie and took some notes.

"As you go through this process, you'll see how to use your house as an investment. In fact, what we did improved our tax savings. And I should tell you that the term 'investment' is rarely used. Instead, we use 'asset' because you increase your cash flow when you increase your assets. You have to shift your valuable house into a profitable asset."

"I can't wait to hear more about that one," said Sam.

"Rule number six is to protect your family. To be honest, this took me some time to understand. This rule, like the rule about not losing money, can go different ways. At first, I translated this rule into the need for insurance. Yes, that's important. But what about the basic fact of designing your assets to generate income you can control?"

"I don't know," Sam said and took a drink of water.

"Remember the Cashflow Quadrant? Shifting to the I Quadrant is important. By doing this, I fulfilled this rule's intention."

"And I guess I did that myself by buying rental properties," Sam said.

"Right," Jim said.

"Rule number seven is to increase your ability to earn. This rule is an accumulation of some of the previous rules. By designing my assets to increase my ability to earn, I can control the previous rules and minimize the effects of not following them. By designing an asset-building plan, all the previous rules automatically put this rule into gear."

Sam said, "I can see that. I see these rules are important because they keep things simple. The practicality in these rules is perfect for what most of us want to accomplish."

"That is what I thought, too. *The eighth rule is to reduce tax liability* and isn't in the book. You'll see it should be. When reviewing all the previous rules, you encompass all previous seven rules by adding this one rule."

Sam looked at his watch. They had been talking for two hours. "Wow. Time flies! I need to get home, but I want to meet again to find out if I can be helped."

Jim replied, "Oh, you can be helped. In fact, you'll find that your business will improve once you go through the process. Well, it was great spending this time together. When did you want to meet up again?"

Sam responded, "As soon as possible. How about I swing by your office in a couple of days, so we can have lunch?"

Jim replied, "It probably makes more sense for us to meet with Kevin, who has been helping me with everything I shared with you. How about I give him a call and schedule time for us to meet with him in a couple of days?"

"Great, shoot me over the details in a text. Thank you. It's been great to see you, Jim."

"Great to see you too!"

. . .

Read the rest of the story in my first book:
**Economic Termites: Protect Your Assets
from Financial Destruction**

Acknowledgments

I'd like to thank my wife, Sara, for believing and trusting in me during this journey. I'd also like to thank my three kids (Isaac, Jordan "JoJo", and Hannah) for acting like what I say is interesting. Lastly, I'd like to thank God for allowing me to be part of His business and letting me guide His ship.

About the Author

ROBERT WOLF has been assisting business owners and high-income taxpayers since 2001.

Robert is an Asset Coach & Tax Strategist. As an Asset Coach & Tax Strategist he successfully reduces his clients' tax liability by organizing and structuring their assets by understanding the guidelines the IRS has for each asset in their respective stages of cash flow and wealth accumulation.

Linkedin: linkedin.com/in/assetcoachtaxstrategist
Facebook: https://www.facebook.com/TerraFirmaConsultants
YouTube: @assetcoachtaxstrategist9468
Website: www.terrafirmaconsultant.com

https://www.youtube.com/channel/UCRF-ckPpqG7OqGwL_x-k1mQ

LISTENER'S FAVORITE EPISODES

California Considers Doubling Its Taxes:

Is China Losing Steam:

Bye Bye California – The "Texodus" Continues:

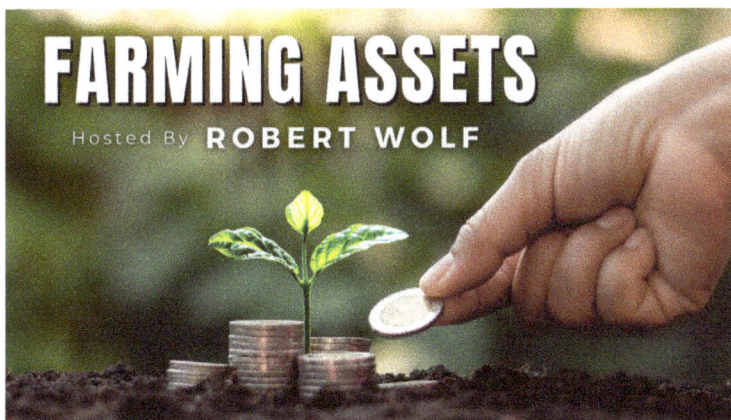

The Farming Assets PodCast

https://podcasts.apple.com/us/podcast/farming-assets/id1638164192

LISTENER'S FAVORITE EPISODES

Mindset of a Business Owner Today:

The Number 1 Asset:

Bye Bye California:

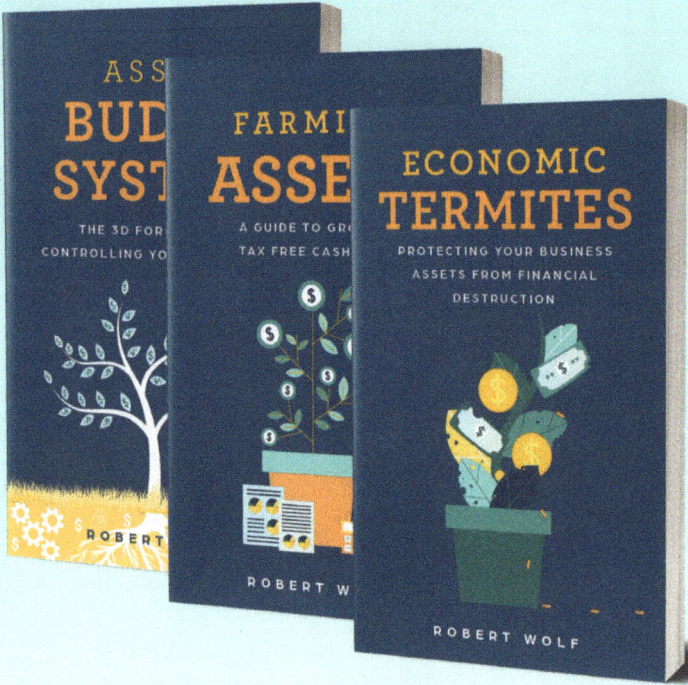

ASS
BUD
SYST

THE 3D FOR
CONTROLLING YO

ROBERT

FARMI
ASSE

A GUIDE TO GR
TAX FREE CASH

ROBERT W

ECONOMIC
TERMITES

PROTECTING YOUR BUSINESS
ASSETS FROM FINANCIAL
DESTRUCTION

ROBERT WOLF

THE
WOLF
FINANCIAL
TRILOGY

Read More
from the Financial Trilogy!

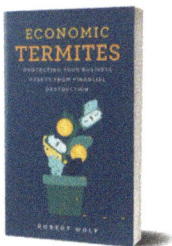

Book 1: Economic Termites

This is a great book to begin the baseline understanding of the issues which silently eat away at your wealth. I walk through the four major economic termites by bringing awareness to what they do and how to exterminate them.

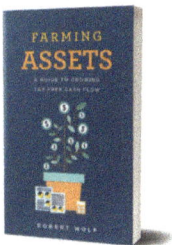

Book 2: Farming Assets

The second book in this series highlights some of the issues brought up in Economic Termites but then explains the next steps of which assets are beneficial in the extermination of those pesky economic termites. Understanding which assets and the type of income generated from those assets brings to light the ability to start building tax free income.

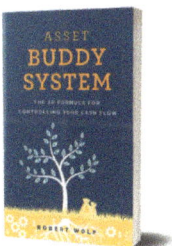

Book 3: Asset Buddy System

The final book in this trilogy is your how-to handbook of what assets to use and how to organize them to put in place an automatic economic termites extermination system. You will learn how to organize which assets to create that tax free income stream that has been elusive to so many Americans.

The books are available at www.terrafirmaconsultant.com and your favorite online book retailers

Leave a Review!

For a self-published author like myself, reviews mean the world! Please write an honest review on the platform from which you purchased this book. I read every one!

Thank you.

♥

www.ingramcontent.com/pod-product-compliance
Lightning Source LLC
Chambersburg PA
CBHW040929210326
41597CB00030B/5231